LIGHTNING BOLT BOOKS™

D1200911

Can You Tell a Triceratops from a Protoceratops?

Buffy Silverman

Lerner Publications Company

Minneapolis

To Jon
(who I locked horns
with for many
childhood years!)
—B.S.

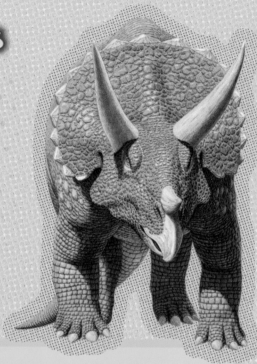

Lerner Publications Company
A division of Lerner Publishing Group, Inc.
241 First Avenue North
Minneapolis, MN 55401 U.S.A.

Website address: www.lernerbooks.com

Library of Congress Cataloging-in-Publication Data

Silverman, Buffy.
    Can you tell a triceratops from a protoceratops? / by Buffy Silverman.
        pages   cm. — (Lightning bolt books™—Dinosaur look-alikes)
    Includes index.
    ISBN 978–1–4677–1357–3 (library binding : alkaline paper)
    ISBN 978–1–4677–1758–8 (eBook)
    1. Triceratops—Juvenile literature. 2. Protoceratops—Juvenile literature. 3. Dinosaurs—Juvenile literature. I. Title.
    QE862.O65S564 2014
    567.915—dc23   2013001104

Manufactured in the United States of America
1 — BP — 7/15/13

Table of Contents

staying safe

Dinosaurs faced many dangers. Special body parts helped them stay safe. Some dinos grew sharp horns. Some had bony plates called frills.

A frill covers the neck of this dinosaur.

Dinosaurs with frills belonged to a group called Ceratopsia. Ceratopsia ate plants. They had sharp beaks.

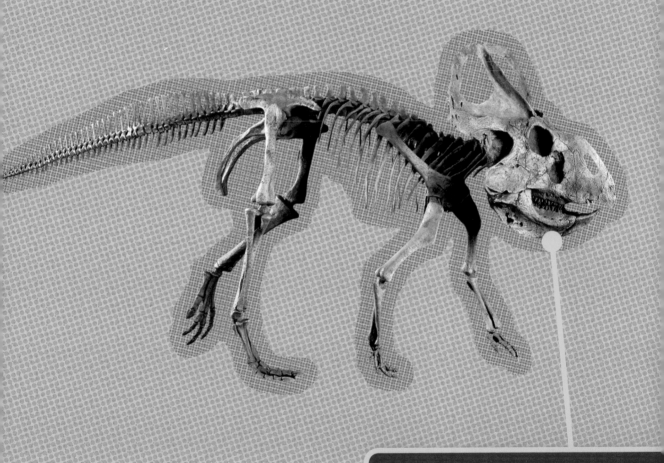

Ceratopsia beaks tore thick leaves from plants.

Ceratopsia had rows of teeth with sawlike edges. They sliced leaves.

Cutting leaves made teeth dull. Worn teeth fell out. New teeth replaced them.

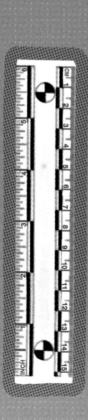

Protoceratops and Triceratops were Ceratopsia. They both had beaks and frills. But you can tell these dinosaurs apart.

Which Ceratopsia is a Protoceratops, and which is a Triceratops?

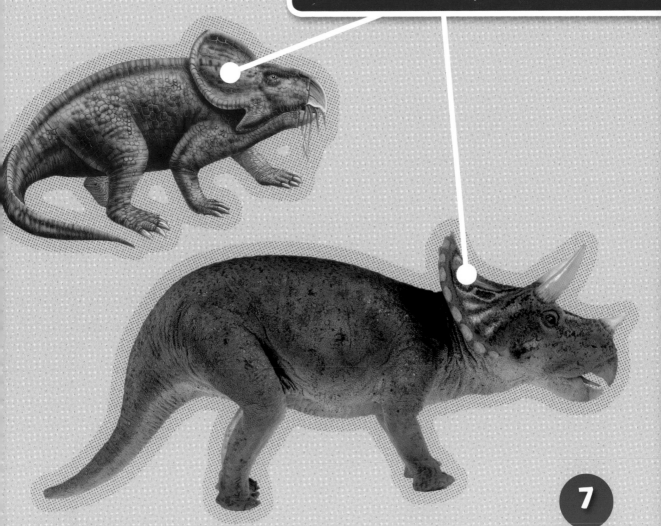

Triceratops had a thick, solid frill. The frill protected its neck from claws and jaws. The frill might also have heated up in the sun. That would have helped Triceratops stay warm.

Protoceratops had a thin frill with two large holes. Skin most likely covered the frill. The frill might have helped attract mates. It also might have helped Protoceratops recognize one another.

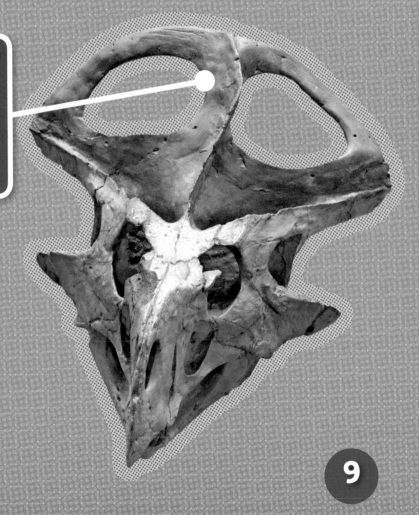

Protoceratops's frill was probably too thin to protect its neck.

Horns or Bumps

Ceratopsia means "horned faces." Some Ceratopsia had two horns on their heads.

Others had three or five horns. Some did not have any horns.

Triceratops had three horns. Two huge horns grew above each eye. A shorter horn grew on its snout.

Triceratops means "three-horned face."

Triceratops probably fought with its horns. A Triceratops horn fossil has been found with teeth marks. A Tyrannosaurus bit the horn.

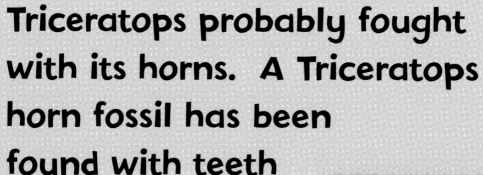

Horns did not always scare off enemies.

Triceratops probably also battled one another. They might have fought over mates.

Protoceratops did not have any horns. Instead, it had a bump on its snout. Males probably had larger bumps than females.

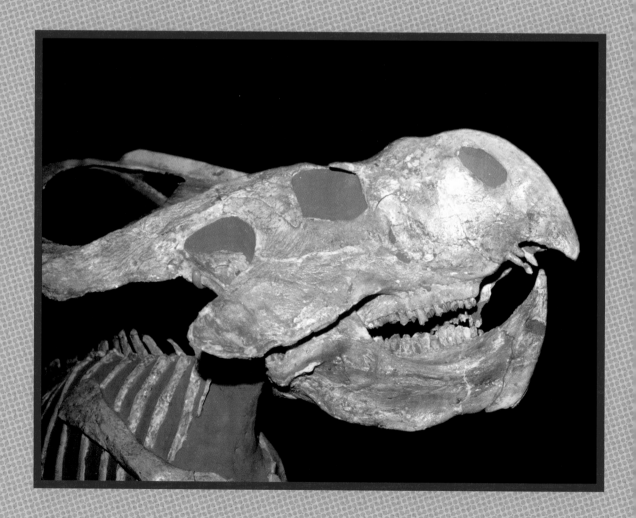

Thick bones grew above Protoceratops's eyes. The bones were in the same spot as Triceratops's horns. *Protoceratops* means "first horned face."

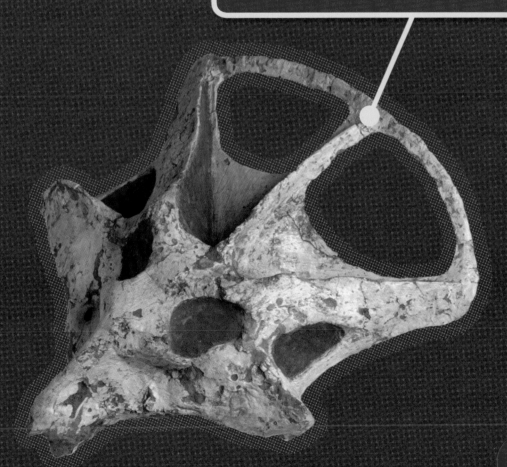

Protoceratops was one of the first Ceratopsia.

Big or Small

Protoceratops was smaller than many horned dinosaurs. It was the size of a sheep.

Triceratops grew about five times larger than Protoceratops. It was longer than an elephant.

This skeleton stands at 25 feet (7.6 meters) long.

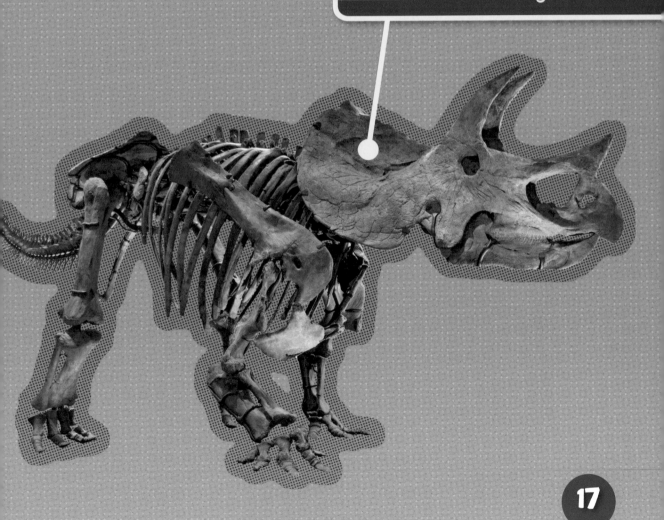

Place and Time

Protoceratops lived millions of years before people. It lived several million years before Triceratops too. It roamed Earth 71 to 75 million years ago.

Triceratops was one of the last dinosaurs on Earth. It lived 65 to 68 million years ago.

Protoceratops fossils have been discovered in Asia. Protoceratops lived in the deserts of Mongolia.

Triceratops lived in the western United States and Canada. People have found their bones in North America.

This skeleton stands at a museum in Alberta, Canada.

Alone or Together

Protoceratops traveled in groups called herds. Fossils of their nests, eggs, and bones of many sizes have been found together.

Fossils are the remains of animals or plants from long ago. These are egg fossils.

Living in a herd kept dinosaurs safe. Everyone watched for predators. They warned one another of danger.

Protoceratops run as a Velociraptor watches from above.

Scientists think Triceratops lived alone. Triceratops fossils are not often found in groups.

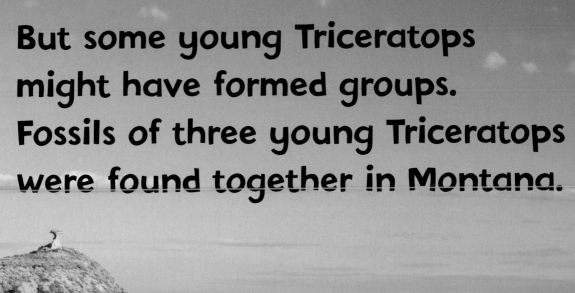

But some young Triceratops might have formed groups. Fossils of three young Triceratops were found together in Montana.

Triceratops once roamed Montana.

Scientists found fossils of fifteen young Protoceratops together. The fifteen youngsters faced the same direction. They might have turned away from blowing sand.

The dinosaurs were huddled in their nest. They were larger than newly hatched Protoceratops. So maybe they grew up in the nest. These fossils might show that Protoceratops cared for their young.

Dino Diagrams

Can you tell these dinosaurs apart?

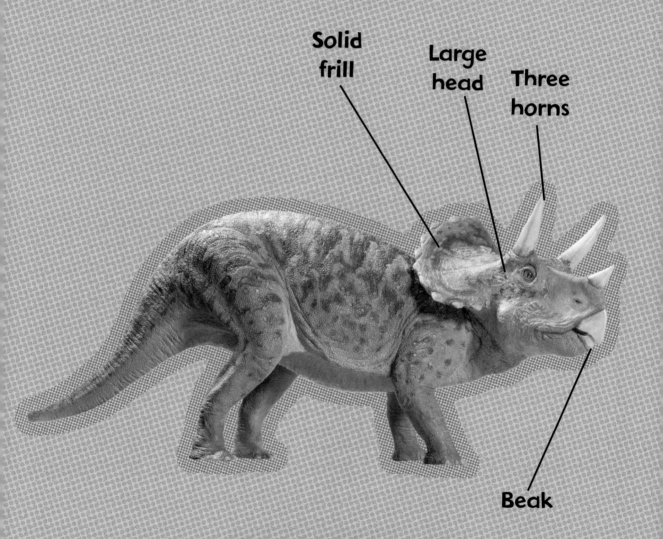

Solid frill

Large head

Three horns

Beak

Triceratops

Protoceratops

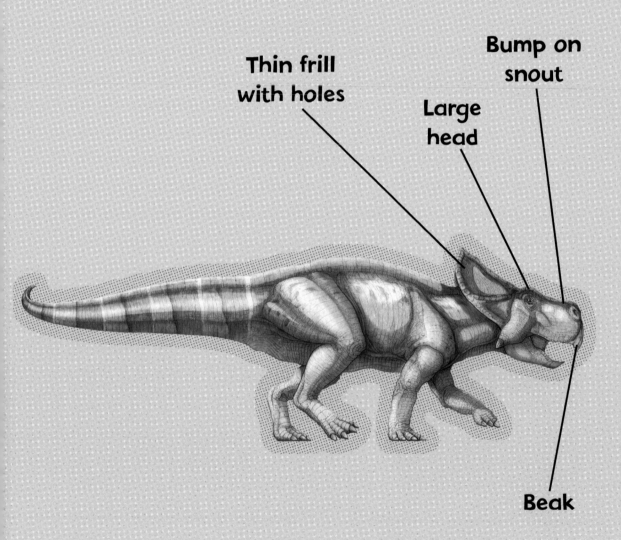

Thin frill
with holes

Large
head

Bump on
snout

Beak

Glossary

Ceratopsia: plant-eating dinosaurs with beaks, frills, and sometimes horns

fossil: the remains of a living thing from a long time ago

frill: a bony plate behind the skull

horn: a solid, usually pointed structure that sticks out from the head of an animal

predator: an animal that hunts other animals

snout: nose and jaws sticking out from an animal's head

Further Reading

Brecke, Nicole, and Patricia M. Stockland. *Dinosaurs and Other Prehistoric Creatures You Can Draw.* Minneapolis: Millbrook Press, 2010.

Creature Features: Triceratops Horridus http://kids.nationalgeographic.com/kids/animals /creaturefeature/triceratops-horridus

Landau, Elaine. *Triceratops.* New York: Children's Press, 2007.

Lessem, Don. *National Geographic Kids Ultimate Dinopedia: The Most Complete Dinosaur Reference Ever.* Washington, DC: National Geographic, 2010.

Prehistoric Life: Immortal Combat http://www.bbc.co.uk/nature/life/Protoceratops #p00clsng

Prehistoric Life: Triceratops Attack http://www.bbc.co.uk/nature/life/Triceratops #p00cjhp1

West, David. *Triceratops and Other Horned Herbivores.* New York: Gareth Stevens Publishing, 2011.

Index

Photo Acknowledgments

The images in this book are used with the permission of: © Stephen J Krasemann/All Canada Photos/Alamy, p. 1 (top); © Richard T. Nowitz/CORBIS, p. 1 (bottom); © Dorling Kindersley RF/Thinkstock, pp. 2, 4; © Francois Gohier/Science Source, p. 5; AP Photo/Guernsey's, p. 6; © De Agostini Picture Library/Getty Images, pp. 7 (top), 10 (top); © Gary Kevin/Dorling Kindersley/Getty Images, p. 7; © Colin Keates/Dorling Kindersley/Getty Images, pp. 8, 15; © Ivan Vdovin/Alamy, p. 9; © Ozja/Shutterstock.com, pp. 10 (bottom), 30; © Millard H. Sharp/Science Source, p. 11; © Gow27/Shutterstock.com, p. 12; © Mark Hallett Paleoart/Science Source, p. 13; © Albert Copley/Visuals Unlimited, Inc., p. 14; © Kevin Schafer/CORBIS, p. 16; © Ambient Images Inc./SuperStock, p. 17; © Charles R. Knight/National Geographic Society/CORBIS, p. 18; © Mario Kessler/dieKleinert/Alamy, p. 19; © Louie Psihoyos/CORBIS p. 20; © Paul Souders/CORBIS, p. 21; © Ken Lucas/Visuals Unlimited, Inc., p. 22; © Mark Steveson/Stocktreck Images/CORBIS, p. 23; AP Photo/Smithsonian National Museum of Natural History, p. 24; © John Reddy/Alamy, p. 25; © De Agostini/SuperStock, p. 26; © Giuliano Fornari/Getty Images, p. 27; © Dave King/Dorling Kindersley/Getty Images, p. 28; © Encyclopaedia Britannica/UIG via Getty Images, p. 29.

Front cover: © Leonello Calvetti/Dreamstime.com (top); © Andreas Meyer/Dreamstime.com (bottom).

Main body text set in Johann Light 30/36.